PLAYER'S POKER

SONGBOOK

Lyrics by

HAUS PLAYER

Table Of Contents

NOTES

HOUSE RULES

Play Friendly

Guard Your Cards

Wait Your Turn

No Free Flops

Mind Your Manners

No Cry Babies

Clean Up Your Mess

Check Yourself Out

GENERAL RULES OF THE GAMES

Dealer's choice of a game - same game is played until it reaches the Dealer - the deck is then passed to the next player who calls a new game.

Dealer antes $1.

Player to the right of the Dealer has the option to cut the deck.

Cards are dealt clockwise.

In the event of a misdeal the players may call for a new deal or the exposed card may be set aside and the last card in the round replaces it.

First rounds of betting have a minimum of 25 cents and a maximum of $2.

All raises must either match the original bet or any higher amount up to $2.

Maximum of 3 raises after the original bet.

3 raise maximum is waived if there are only two players left (head-to-head).

All bets must be clearly displayed

- no splashing the pot.

Betting is always clockwise, and each player must wait their turn to declare action.

All hands in play must be clearly visible.

The "Bet or Get" Dealer may declare "bet or get" when the game has an initial card dealt face up. The Dealer declares the amount and whether it applies to the highest or lowest card. Aces are always the starting bet either way. If the player "gets" (folds), then the next player has the option to "bet or get."

The bet option is the set minimum or a higher amount - not to exceed $2.

The final betting round action starts with the highest hand showing.

A player who does not have enough chips to call or raise a bet has four options:

1. Buy more chips from the house or from another player to continue the round.
2. Go "all in" and place their remaining chips in the pot. A side pot is then set up between the remaining players, with the all-in amount staying in the main pot. All subsequent bets go to the side pot.
3. "Go Light" Draw chips from the pot equal to the amount bet and place them in front of you.

At the showdown:

-If you are the winner, you may take your lights and the pot.

-If you are the loser, then you must throw in chips or cash equal to your lights.

- If you split the pot, then give your lights to the other winning player before splitting the pot.

4. Fold.

Rules Committee

GAMES

Following the rules

Is how every game is played:

Rules are not equal

OMAHA EIGHT (POSOE)

Deal four cards to each player.

Split pot high/low with an 8 qualifier for low.

The player may use any 2 (and only 2) of the cards in their hand to make a high or low. The player may go both ways with the same card.

Exp: Three of the cards are King - Ace - 2: low Is possible with Ace - 2, and high is possible with Ace-King, or Ace-2 could be played high (or both ways) if they are suited.

After the first betting round,

The Dealer turns over 3 community cards (burn optional). Each Dealer has a burn option, but they must be consistent.

After the flop betting round, the Dealer turns one community card (Turn).

After the betting round, the Dealer turns one community card (River).

Last betting round - the maximum bet is $5.

GREATER OMAHA EIGHT

Same split game as Omaha Eight, except 5 cards are dealt to each player, and they may use any combination of two along with three from the board to make a hand.

OHAMA SLUTS

Same as Greater Omaha Eight, only each player must turn up one of the five cards and place it near his hand. This is the slut card, and it may be used as part of the other board cards giving the player Six board cards. Betting action is the highest hand showing.

POSOE LOCO

Same as Omaha Eight with the rule change that the player must play at least 2 cards from their hand.

This means they can play up to 4 cards, but they must play at least 2. Option - Low qualifier is 7.

OMAHA EIGHT DOUBLE FLOP

Same as Omaha Eight; only after betting ends on the first flop a second flop is made.

TEXAS HOLD 'EM

The game is usually played as high only. Each player is dealt two cards down.

First hand must bet 50 cents (blind) Second hand must bet $1 (big blind)

The big blind has the option to raise or stay if no raises are made

Community cards are then dealt (3-1-1) with a round of betting after each deal

Burn Option: Dealer may discard the top card on each round. After this choice is made the Dealer must be consistent with the next two community cards.

First community deal is three cards (the Flop)
Second community deal is one card (the Turn)
Third community deal is one card (the River)

Final round of betting with a $5 maximum.

TEXAS HOLD-UP

Same as Texas Hold 'em except each player is dealt an extra card up, and there are no blinds.

Betting action is by the highest card(s) showing.

PINEAPPLE

Same as Texas Hold 'em, except players are each dealt three cards. After the first round of betting, and before the flop, each remaining player must discard one card, converting to regular Texas Hold 'em rules.

BI-NAPPLE

Same as Pineapple, except each player has the option of paying 50 cents to keep the third card prior to the flop. After the flop betting round, all players must be down to two cards, and the game proceeds as regular Texas Hold 'Em.

SUPER DUPER BI-NAPPLE

Same as Bi-Napple, except after the flop betting and before the turn, any player with three cards may declare they want to keep the third card and pay $1 to the pot.

The turn card betting round is made.

Players who wish to keep the third card for the River must declare so and pay $2.

8

After the River card is turned up and before the final betting round, any player still holding a third card must now discard or pay $4 to use all three cards at the showdown.

Final betting round with the $5 individual bet limit.

At the showdown, the player holding 3 cards and having paid $7.50 may play them all.

Colossal Eight: High/Low Super Duper Bi-Napple split pot with an 8 qualifier.

FIVE CARD DRAW - JACKS OR BACK

5 cards are dealt face down to each player.

Any player with a pair of Jacks or better may open.

After the betting round, the players may draw up to three cards
- four cards if the player shows an Ace.

Last betting round with the highest hand winning.

No one opens with Jacks or better?

— The game becomes lowball.

Straights and flushes do not count in lowball. The straight Ace through Five is the nut low.

After the betting round, each player may draw up to three cards - four cards if the player shows an Ace.

Last betting round with the lowest hand winning.

Betting Option: Because there are only two rounds of betting, the Dealer may increase the betting limits with the approval of all players.

LOWBALL TRIPLE DRAW

The lowest hand wins, A-5 is the nut.
Straights and flushes do not count.
Variations: Six/four or Seven/Five is nut low (ace is high) - Straights and flushes are high.
Each player is dealt five cards face down –
Betting round.
Each player may draw up to three cards –
Betting round.

Each player may draw up to two cards - Betting round.

Each player may draw one card - Betting round. Showdown.

BADUGI

Four four-card lowball game with blinds.

Objective: Obtain the lowest unsuited/unpaired hand.

Each player is dealt 4 cards down.

After the first betting round, players may discard any or all of their cards, and the Dealer replaces them player by player.

This pattern repeats for two more betting rounds. No 4-card hand? Then, the best 3 card hand wins. Ace is the lowest card. Lowest high card wins.

EIGHTY-THREE

Standard seven-card stud.

Split pot game with qualifiers for both high and low. High must be at least three-of-a-kind or higher, and the low hand must be no higher than 8 (straights and flushes do not disqualify a low hand).

If there is no qualifying low, then the highest hand wins the pot.

If there is no qualifying high but a low hand is made, then the low hand wins the pot.

No qualifying high hand or low hand - the highest hand wins the pot.

LOW HOLE CARD WILD

Deal standard 7 card stud.

The lowest down card is wild, and any other cards of the same value are also wild.

Betting begins with the highest card showing.

Three more cards are dealt with a betting round after each card.

Last down card options:

Player who called the game may declare insurance for the final card. Players who take the option receive their final card face up. The amount of insurance must be declared at the start - usual amount is $4 or $5.

Player who called the game may declare no insurance and all players received the last card face down.

Highest hand is five of a kind.

LOW/HIGH CHICAGO

Seven-card stud game for up to eight players.
The Dealer declares either the high or low spade
dealt face down will split the pot with the highest
hand
The lowest spade is the two, and the highest is
the ace.

RED HOLD 'EM / OMAHA

Played exactly like the regular games, but the
river card must be red. If the river card is black,
then the deal and betting rounds - Max $2 -
continue until a red card is turned up.
Both games have blinds and are high only.

SHUCK TWO OR NONE

Six card stud - two down and four up.
Split pot game with no qualifiers. The highest
card showing has the action. Bet each round
until 4 cards are up.
After the 4th betting round ends, each player,
starting with the last raiser, must declare a

SHUCK 2 or stay with the hand they have.

Shuck players must exchange any two cards for fresh cards.

Dealer deals a single card to each shuck player replacing down cards first.

Another single card is dealt until each player has two down and four up cards.

Last round of betting has an upper limit of $5.

LINN COUNTY SHOTGUN

Up to 10 players.

Split pot stud game - best high/best low - no qualifiers.

Each player is dealt 5 cards face down - Betting round.

The Dealer plays one card face up - Betting round.

The Dealer plays one card face up - Last betting round.

FIVE CARD STUD

All versions start with one card dealt face down and one face up.

Standard: Three additional cards are dealt one at a time face up until each player has five cards.

Maverick: The last card (5th) is dealt face down.

Betting rounds start with:

LOW BALL - lowest card HIGH ONLY - highest card

Option for low ball: Kings are wild

SIX CARD STUD

Same as Five Card Maverick with an additional (4th) up card exposed.

POKER HAIKU

SOUNDS

The sounds of poker
Shuffling cards and clinking ice
Hands smoothing the felt

ADVICE

Speaking for myself
All advice is forgotten
Once the shuffle starts

RUDEST OF HANDS

Nothing uncommon
It has always existed
The rudest of hands

SPECTATOR SPORT

The horse race is set
Raises follow every turn
A spectator sport

MY WISH

I'm wishing myself
A most modest winning streak
Just to even up

NEUTRAL

The cards are neutral
Playing favorites for no one
But they are fickle

PRAY FOR RAIN

You like to gamble
Throwing fortunes to the clouds
And praying for rain

TIME WARP

You want to go back
Rethink what you threw away
Time warp your troubles

IF I HAD WINGS

I wish I had wings
Instead of these puny arms
I'd fly away strong

MISMATCHED

No hands are the same
Shuffled random; cut in half
Mismatched and perfect

ALL I'VE DONE

When will wisdom come
I know it's not by aging
Since that's all I've done

FINGER FUMBLE

The Dealer is drunk
His fingers fumble the deck,
Misdeal me an ace

NO CLEAN UP

The spills that we make

An embarrassment of fate

No clean-up needed

DESPAIR

Despair of the game

That takes your spirit away

It will be returned

THE NUT

Half eaten or raw

the nut is a lovely fruit

When held in your hand

WAKING UP SLOWLY

I woke up slowly

Watching my dreams run away

Or were they stolen?

CON MAN CLUB

Freedom of the press
Has been bought and sold to you
By the Con Man Club

TEA LEAVES

The tea leaves are read
Wise gypsies know their meaning
All others see mud

BABY BOOMER BLUES

Baby Boomer Blues
The unobserved decline
So many lost naps

I HEAR YOU

I hear you calling
A voice in the wilderness
The wolves hear you too

PITCHMAN

The persuasive voice

Urging you to act now, at once

Phone lines are open

PROMISING CLOSURE

The persistent thought

Always looking for closure

Drives my existence

TAKING MY TIME

I'm taking my time

Preparing for the future

Resisting all change

WORK

Sensory deprived

Buried in a cardboard box

Digging out reports

TARGET

You desire gold
A hoarder of finer things
You target yourself

ENTER THE GAME

All eyes peer at you
the unknown hands are waiting
Make your presence known

CALL IT LUCK

The silent partner
A helping hand from above
Don't dare call it luck

WASTED YOUTH

The freedom of youth
Wasted on formalities
And obligations

EASIEST PLAN

The easiest plan

Is to live life as it comes

Trusting all choices

TELL ME

I'm never aware

Of the attempts being made

to tell me something

SOBER TRUTH

The sober truth speaks

When asked about the weather

"Step outside and see"

WHAT I KNOW

Experience gained

I now know with certainty

What I know ain't so

LOST VOICE

The piper has passed

Seven-up Seagram in hand

He once sang with us

FIRST CALLER

Who's in the kitchen
Slowly making a sandwich?
He calls the first bet

HIGHER BRAIN

We can never know
How the higher brain evolved
We are not allowed

LUCK

Luck does not sit still
It weaves and dodges about
Pausing, just briefly

EAGLE GRIP

My cushioned armchair
Holds me gripped like an eagle
Boasting of its prey

CALL IT MONEY

We call it money
Spewed from thousands of presses
Promises to pay

WHAT TO DO

There's no perfect clue

Only the signs and symbols

Placed out of order

COFFIN NAILS

Nails in the coffin

Bad habits that will be used

To keep the lid closed

COSTLY MISTAKE
We laughed at ourselves
thinking luck was a sure thing
A costly mistake

RANDOM RUDENESS

The cards are random

Chosen blindly from the pack

They may be quite rude

DARK SPELL

A dark spell is cast

By a minor poker god

Missing all but me

LUCKY START

I started lucky

Tripping and flushing my hands

Wisecracking wisely

FEW CHOICES

Car radio on

Classic rock or public talk

My choices are few

GROWL

The dramatic fold

A growl of disappointment

A thudding of cards

MILITARY

Motivational

Focused on what needs doing

Sending in rookies

OVERRULE

All gamblers go broke

It's the rule they must follow

Over and over

BUMPER CAR READY

All egos are here

Unbruised and freshly polished

Bumper car ready

WE ARE GATHERED

We are gathered here

To witness futility

Among the fishes

FORTUNE

Your fortune awaits

Held in the hands of others

Who plan to keep it

FIGMENTS

You hide your knowledge

Preferring to act the fool

Spitting out figments

ROUTINE

Old men like routine

The repeated daily chores

Usually Ignored

RECOLLECTIONS

Vague recollections

Picked from gossip and short dreams

Truthfully retold

MADNESS OF FOOLS

The madness of fools

Using charms and magic spells

Seeking nirvana

ONCE UPON A TIME

Once upon a time

The circus was everywhere

Tonight, it is here

MASTER OF MANNERS

Master of manners

Collector of the obscure

We can talk for hours

LESSON NOT LEARNED

The lesson just learned

tucked away insecurely

So soon forgotten

ANONYMOUS MUCK

Another missed chance

Swept away by doubting self

Anonymous muck

SMELL THE CHEESE

Some start out timid

Like mice in a novel maze

They can smell the cheese

A NEW CHANCE

Never surrender

Every deal is a new chance

To plot your revenge

BAD END

Cards with no faces

Unsuited and unfriended

Doomed to a bad end

DEMENTIA

Dementia relapse

half-forgotten memories

From moments ago

GROOMING FOR GREATNESS

Mom in a hurry

Spit baths for everyone

Grooming for greatness!

SOMETHING HALF THOUGHT

sounds are distracting

they take away attention

from something half-thought

GRUMPY

Grumpy had reasons

To complain about Itchy

Sleeping in his bed

NO SCRAPS

Your goose is cooked

No need for a doggy bag

There will be no scraps

MODEST MEN

They hate their places
Modest men with modest means
Wanting so much more

THINGS PICKED HASTILY

We scurry about
Choosing things picked hastily
Running out of time

UNHOLY PAIR

An unholy pair
Has lead me to temptation
The blame is now set

MINEFIELD

Greater Omaha
Cards half seen, half unseen
A mid-west minefield

OBJECT OF THE GAME

I'm playing a game
The object is to stay young
I think I'm losing

ZOMBIE WALK

I stand up slowly
My bones struggle to align
Bathroom zombie walk

WORM ON A HOOK

The worm on the hook
Stretches out and wraps around
Unsure of its fate

STRATEGY PLOTTED

Bet into weakness
Your strategy is plotted
The sandbagger calls

CHEAP STUFF

Corporate mindset
To cultivate the masses
Promise them cheap stuff

BREAKING NEWS

Breaking News Alert
A politician has lied,
Perhaps misspoken

BETWEEN THE DEALS

The score is settled
A peaceable lull follows
A war has begun

WAIT YOUR TURN

Rules of Behavior
No shouting or complaining
while waiting your turn

HANDS IN THE MUCK

Some players drop out

Throwing their hands in the muck

Softly cursing fate

KANSAS

Coyotes roam here

Eating food found on porches

Eyeing small creatures

SKATING

The ice is melting

You may need another drink

Skate to the kitchen

COUNTERFEIT RIVER

Counterfeit River

You dry the bones in my hand

Cracked lips curse the muck

PATTERNS

Patterns in the air

The swirl of cigarette smoke

You cough up your bet

PRETTY GOOD

I had an answer

It was a pretty good one

But it escapes me

A GAME

They call it a game

A social conversation

Arranged around war

ADVISING OTHERS

Advising others

On what they ought to have done

Should be avoided

LAUGH AT LUCK

I don't laugh at luck
Mocking it's brutal choices
It may turn on me

CHECK BET

The emphatic check
the opposite of betting
contradicting bluff

AT THIS TIME

Elemental time
Doled out by obligations
Paused for the moment

PEOPLE SAY

People say I'm short
I must say, I've seen shorter,
Without being rude

CARELESS FLING

When dealing the cards
A careless fling nullifies
The nice things once said

ETERNAL NUT

This is all I want
The undefeatable hand
The eternal nut

THIS IS ALLOWED

Someone is lying;
This is allowed in poker
Getting caught will hurt

SHOE STORE

A shoe store opens
And shuts down your lowball draw
It's not the first time

PROPER GREETING

The proper greeting

The first time you meet someone

Is to tip your hat

MEMORIES

Passing through stages

Shaping some vague memories

Wishing they were true

Poker Night

- by Thomas Hart Benton

GIBBERISH

I don't understand

How to interpret my hand

When it's gibberish

LINN COUNTY SHOTGUN

Linn County Shotgun

Blind dogs barking at the moon,

Scaring off rabbits

LEARNING TO PLAY

We are like children

Learning to play hide and seek

With gauze-covered eyes

OMAHA SLUTS

May I call Omaha sluts?

Eyeballs floating up

The ceiling rule applies here

SIGNS

Signs of growing old

Forgetting names then faces

Impending drivel

LIFE IN A BOX

I live in a box

Arranged for certain comforts

Big enough for two

FAMILY POT

The family pot

occurring infrequently

Let the feuding start

HAPPY ENDING

I like fairy tales

They all have happy endings

Except for the wolf

www.ingramcontent.com/pod-product-compliance
Lightning Source LLC
Chambersburg PA
CBHW051558120626
46551CB00013B/1573

* 9 7 8 1 9 6 4 2 1 0 0 9 4 *